W9-AET-803

Digging Up the Dead

CRYPTS
and TOMBS

By Therese Shea

Gareth Stevens
PUBLISHING

Please visit our website, www.garethstevens.com. For a free color catalog of all our high-quality books, call toll free 1-800-542-2595 or fax 1-877-542-2596.

Library of Congress Cataloging-in-Publication Data

Shea, Therese.
Crypts and tombs / by Therese Shea.
p. cm. — (Digging up the dead)
Includes index.
ISBN 978-1-4824-1277-2 (pbk.)
ISBN 978-1-4824-1225-3 (6-pack)
ISBN 978-1-4824-1483-7 (library binding)
1. Burial — Juvenile literature. 2. Funeral rites and ceremonies — Juvenile literature. I. Shea, Therese. II. Title.
GT3150.S54 2015
393—d23

First Edition

Published in 2015 by
Gareth Stevens Publishing
111 East 14th Street, Suite 349
New York, NY 10003

Copyright © 2015 Gareth Stevens Publishing

Designer: Andrea Davison-Bartolotta
Editor: Greg Roza

Photo credits: Cover, p. 1 Todd Keith/E+/Getty Images; cover, back cover, pp. 1–32 (background dirt texture) Kues/Shutterstock.com; pp. 4, 6, 8, 10, 12, 14, 16, 19, 21, 22, 25, 27, 28 (gravestone) jayfish/Shutterstock.com; p. 4 Tuma/Shutterstock.com; p. 5 Ruggero Giovanni/The Bridgeman Art Library/Getty Images; pp. 6–7 Pecold/Shutterstock.com; p. 7 (inset) DEA/G. Dagli Orti/De Agostini/Getty Images; p. 9 (main) WitR/iStock/Thinkstock; p. 9 (inset) Dorling Kindersley/Getty Images; pp. 10–11 lapas77/Shutterstock.com; p. 11 (inset) contax66/Shutterstock.com; p. 12 (inset) Toshitaka Morita/Sebun Photo/amana images/Getty Images; pp. 12–13 Yoichi Tsukioka/amana images/Getty Images; p. 13 (inset) Tim Kiser/Wikimedia Commons; p. 15 (main) turtix/Shutterstock.com; p. 15 (inset) paul cowell/Shutterstock.com; pp. 16, 16–17 (top) Andreas Solaro/AFP/Getty Images; p. 17 (bottom) © iStockphoto.com/stockcam; pp. 18–19 littlesam/Shutterstock.com; p. 19 (inset) Peter Macdiarmid/Getty Images; pp. 20–21 Patrick Horton/Lonely Planet Images/Getty Images; p. 22 photowind/Shutterstock.com; p. 23 Ivan Drozdov/Shutterstock.com; p. 24 jlawangkun/Shutterstock.com; p. 25 (top) Raymond Boyd/Getty Images; p. 25 (bottom) Kevin Winter/Touchstone Pictures/Getty Images; p. 26 (first) HelleM/Shutterstock.com; p. 26 (second) kavring/Shutterstock.com; p. 26 (third) Evgenia Bolyukh/Shutterstock.com; p. 26 (fourth) Aphichart/Shutterstock.com; p. 27 Spaces Images/Blend Images/Getty Images; pp. 28–29 (map) L.Watcharapol/Shutterstock.com; pp. 28–29 (pins) Aleksandr Bryliaev/Shutterstock.com.

Printed in the United States of America

CPSIA compliance information: Batch #CS15GS: For further information contact Gareth Stevens, New York, New York at 1-800-542-2595.

CONTENTS

Words in the glossary appear in **bold** type
the first time they are used in the text.

CREEPY CRYPTS AND TERRIFYING TOMBS?

Some of the scariest movies have a graveyard scene. Perhaps a dead body suddenly comes to life in a crypt or a skeleton pops out of a tomb to grab the hero. These things can't happen in real life, but crypts and tombs really do hold dead bodies.

A crypt is a chamber, partly or completely underground, where people are buried. Crypts are often found in old graveyards and beneath old churches. A tomb is a space, chamber, or building in which a dead body is kept. So, a crypt may also be called a tomb, but an aboveground tomb isn't a crypt. Both can look very different, as you'll see in this book, but all serve as final resting places. While that might seem creepy, many famous tombs are interesting and beautiful monuments.

ruins of the Mausoleum of Halicarnassus

GRAVE MATTERS

In Latin, *crypta* was a word used for any vaulted building partially or entirely below the ground. This included sewers and cellars.

Mausoleums

A mausoleum (maw-suh-LEE-uhm) is a supertomb! Historically, a mausoleum is a large, decorated building that's meant to be a tomb as well as a monument to honor the dead. The word comes from *Mausolus*, the name of a ruler in ancient Turkey. Around 350 BC, his wife had a tomb built for him that became one of the Seven Wonders of the World. People still build mausoleums today, but they aren't quite as large or impressive as this one was.

Though the Mausoleum of Halicarnassus (haa-luh-kahr-NAA-suhs), as Mausolus's tomb is called, is now in ruins, ancient historians recorded details about it.

NEWGRANGE

Newgrange in Ireland was built around 3200 BC. It's actually a burial mound, meaning it's a hill of stone and soil constructed over the remains of the dead. That might not sound remarkable, but this hill is 250 feet (76 m) across and 40 feet (12 m) high! The workers built a tunnel under the mound that leads to a vaulted burial chamber.

Archaeologists believe the tunnel of Newgrange was constructed to mark the shortest day of the year, December 21, in a special way. On that day, the sun is in the right position to shine through an opening above the entrance. It lights up the whole tunnel and inner burial chamber. Why Newgrange was built like this and who is buried there are still mysteries.

GRAVE MATTERS

Many people in Ireland enter a lottery each year to be able to stand inside Newgrange on December 21. In 2013, 30,000 people entered, but only 50 were chosen.

tunnel of Newgrange

Why Underground?

Have you ever wondered why people bury the dead? Many ancient peoples believed that the afterlife, or life after death, was under the ground. Burial was a way of placing the dead closer to the afterlife. Many were buried with things it was thought they might want, such as weapons, pets, and money. When Queen Puabi of **Mesopotamia** died around 2334 BC, she was buried with 60 servants. They were killed so they could serve her in the afterlife!

Besides being an ancient example of a tomb, some think Newgrange is the oldest building in the world!

THE PYRAMIDS OF GIZA

Found on the west bank of the Nile River in northern Egypt, the Pyramids of Giza were built between 2575 BC and 2465 BC as the final resting places of three kings, or pharaohs: Khufu (KOO-foo), Khafre (KAF-ray), and Menkaure (mehn-KOW-ray).

Khufu's pyramid, made of 2.3 million stone blocks, is the largest. It's called the Great Pyramid. Tunnels through the structure lead to three rooms, including the king's chamber where Khufu was likely buried. His stone coffin, or sarcophagus (sahr-KAH-fuh-guhs), is too big to fit through the tunnels, so it must have been placed before the pyramid's top was completed.

Khufu's body is missing, however, as is much of the treasure he was buried with. People have been looting, or stealing from, the pyramids since ancient times.

GRAVE MATTERS

Several mysterious tunnels that aren't big enough to be hallways lead from the Great Pyramid's inner chambers. It's thought they may have been made to allow Khufu's spirit to roam.

The Giza Necropolis

Even before the Pyramids of Giza were built, many pharaohs and other nobles were buried in this area. That's why it's called a necropolis, which means "city of the dead" in Greek. In fact, Khufu moved tombs in order to raise his pyramid. How these gigantic pyramids were built has long been a mystery, but archaeologists now think workers rolled stone blocks up ramps. A workers' village was unearthed nearby as well as their tombs.

Khufu's Pyramid

king's chamber

grand gallery

queen's chamber

underground chamber

Khufu's Pyramid

The Great Pyramid used to be about 481 feet (147 m) high. Now it's about 30 feet (9 m) shorter because the outer layer of limestone was stripped away to help build the nearby city of Cairo.

THE TOMB OF CHINA'S FIRST EMPEROR

China was once made up of different territories, one of which was the state of Qin (CHIN). Qin began to conquer neighboring states and, by 221 BC, its ruler—also named Qin—had established an empire and declared himself its first emperor. (The word "China" comes from the name "Qin.")

Emperor Qin's incredible mausoleum is actually a burial complex, which means it consists of many sections. One room contained around 8,000 life-sized soldiers made of baked reddish clay called terra-cotta. Other chambers include a stable of horses and a zoo.

GRAVE MATTERS

Each of the terra-cotta soldiers has a different face. They were also painted, but the colors have worn off. They were armed with real weapons, too!

The inner tomb has yet to be **excavated**. It lies under a pyramid and is thought to house an entire palace as well as a river of poisonous **mercury**. The Chinese government is likely waiting until there are better ways of protecting what's inside.

The Destructive Science of Archaeology

Just opening the Qin tomb and exposing it to air or sunlight is a risk. After so many years, buried materials can become very delicate. Early archaeologists uncovering sites in Egypt destroyed much in their efforts to unearth treasures. Today's archaeologists work very slowly, digging gently and using brushes layer after layer to make sure they don't miss anything. It's thought that robots might be sent to look at Qin's tomb first!

terra-cotta horses

Found in 1974, the first emperor of China's tomb will be explored for many years to come. It's thought that it took 700,000 workers more than 36 years to construct it!

13

NINTOKU'S TOMB

Like Newgrange in Ireland, the Qin tomb is a burial mound because it was covered with a mass of stone and dirt. Another famous, and incredibly large, burial mound is the tomb of the 4th-century Japanese emperor Nintoku, located near the city of Osaka. About 1,594 feet (486 m) long and 115 feet (35 m) high, it's made up of a keyhole-shaped mound surrounded by water. This was a style of burial mound, also called a tumulus (TOO-myuh-luhs), popular for rulers of the time in Japan.

Nintoku's tomb is located in the rounded part of the mound. Special ceremonies for the dead would have taken place in the lower part of the shape. The moat, or water-filled ditch, was dug around the area to protect the grave.

GRAVE MATTERS

From the entrance to Nintoku's tomb, it just looks like a forest. You can only tell what shape it is from above.

In Japan, the bigger the tumulus, the more powerful the leader. Nintoku's tomb is the largest of its kind.

Adena Burial Mounds

Burial mounds were an important part of some Native American traditions. The Adena of the Ohio Valley (800 BC to AD 100) are famous for their burial mounds. Early mounds were simple, with the dead laid on bark and covered by dirt. Later mounds contained rooms with painted bodies as well as jewelry, food, and other objects. Grave Creek Mound in West Virginia contains multiple burials, which is why it's 69 feet (21 m) high.

TAJ MAHAL

The Taj Mahal in Agra, India, is a five-domed, white marble mausoleum constructed between 1631 and 1648. **Mughal** emperor Shah Jahan ordered it built for his favorite wife, Mumtaz Mahal. It's considered one of the most beautiful buildings in the world because of its **symmetry** and many fine details, such as the placement into walls of colored stones cut into the shape of flowers. A garden divided into four sections by long pools of water was raised around the structure.

The tomb of Mumtaz Mahal is found in the south side of the building. It was placed on a square platform with a series of steps leading up to it. But she's not buried there! She and Shah Jahan are buried in crypts below. False tombs weren't unusual for this time period.

GRAVE MATTERS

Empty tombs, such as the ones in the Taj Mahal, are called cenotaphs (SEH-nuh-tafs).

The white marble of the Taj Mahal reflects the colors of the sky. In turn, the building is reflected in the pools around it.

Humayun's Tomb

The Taj Mahal was inspired by an earlier garden-tomb. Built in 1570, Humayun's Tomb in Delhi, India, was the first example of this kind of **architecture**. It features a mixture of ideas from Persia (today called Iran) and India. The huge structure was built for the second emperor of the Mughal empire, Humayun. His wife, Biga Begum, had it built about 14 years after his death. It's located in the center of a garden divided into four parts. Other family members are also buried there.

ROMAN CATACOMBS

There's another world underneath the city of Rome, Italy. It's not a world for the living. Hundreds of miles of tunnels were excavated to house the remains of the dead, some dating back to the second century AD. Jews and early Christians buried their dead under the city, sometimes adding artwork to the walls and ceilings. The living also spent time down there. Rooms with benches were thought to be places where people would bring food to eat with their dead loved ones. "Picnics with the dead" were common.

After the **catacombs** were looted in the 700s and 800s, many of the remains of the dead were brought to the surface and reburied or placed in churches. Gradually, the catacombs were forgotten, but they were rediscovered in the 1500s.

inside the Roman catacombs

GRAVE MATTERS

There may be catacombs in Rome that haven't been discovered yet.

Some of the oldest images linked to the young Christian religion were discovered in the Roman catacombs in 2010.

A Second Tomb

Paris, France, also has hundreds of miles of catacombs beneath it. The tunnels were initially excavated by Romans because they were a good place to find stone for building. However, in the 1700s and 1800s, many people's remains were removed from graveyards to make room for the newly dead.

They were then dumped into the tunnels. About 6 million people's remains are thought to be located in the Parisian ossuary, a term which means a vault to hold the bones of the dead.

WESTMINSTER ABBEY

Westminster Abbey is a well-known church in London, England, where the British monarchs have been crowned for hundreds of years. It's also where many British rulers, artists, scientists, and other important figures are buried. These include scientists Isaac Newton and Charles Darwin. Poets' Corner is a part of the church where author Geoffrey Chaucer, poet Robert Browning, and many other writers are buried.

There are about 450 tombs and monuments in Westminster Abbey.

Some of the tombs are raised, while others are under the floor. There is just one tomb on which visitors aren't allowed to step. This is the resting place of the Unknown Warrior—an unidentified soldier from World War I. A similar tomb exists in Arlington National Cemetery in Virginia. These tombs have come to represent all soldiers whose remains haven't been claimed or found.

the monument of Queen Elizabeth I and Queen Mary

Together Forever

Queen Elizabeth I was the last monarch buried at Westminster to have a monument built above her crypt. It's an **effigy** of the long-serving queen. Interestingly, during her life, Elizabeth and her older sister Mary were at odds. Mary was queen first and had Elizabeth imprisoned for a while, fearing she would seize the throne. However, their brother had both their bodies placed in the same tomb. Latin words written nearby call them "partners in throne and grave."

GRAVE MATTERS

A political leader from the 1600s named Oliver Cromwell *was* buried in the abbey. However, his remains were later removed and hung, and his head was displayed on a pole for many years!

19

CITY OF THE DEAD

Imagine going into a tomb—and staying there until you die. That's not just a bad nightmare; it was a reality for some people in Russia. Dargavs lies in a beautiful valley marked by a number of white stone huts. It looks like a pretty village. If you were to look inside one of those huts, though, you'd see bones—each is a tomb!

It's believed that villagers used these huts as family tombs. The story goes that, in the 1700s, a terrible plague swept through the region. To keep it from spreading, the sick entered the tombs themselves—even with other dead bodies inside. They were given food and water until they died. Today, this place is called the City of the Dead.

It's very hard to reach Dargavs. It's about a 3-hour drive from the nearest city through the mountains.

Boats Without a River

Some of the bodies at Dargavs are laid in small, wooden slabs shaped like boats. Since there are no rivers nearby that can be traveled by boat, it was a mystery at first why these would be important enough to place in the tombs. However, archaeologists now know that the people buried there believed that a soul had to cross a river to reach heaven. The boats were supposed to help them achieve their goal.

GRAVE MATTERS

Part of the legend of the City of the Dead is that no one who walked in would come out alive.

LENIN'S MAUSOLEUM

Not all tombs are from hundreds or thousands of years ago. And not all tombs conceal the body inside! The tomb of Vladimir Lenin in Moscow, Russia, actually displays the body for visitors. Lenin helped create the **communist** Soviet Union and was head of state from 1917 to 1924. When he died in 1924, his body was embalmed, which means it was treated with chemicals to preserve it and stop it from decaying. Then it was placed in a mausoleum in Moscow's Red Square for all to see.

The mausoleum is in the shape of a pyramid with steps. It's made of black, gray, and red granite and is positioned in front of the Kremlin, which is the center of Russian government.

Lenin

GRAVE MATTERS

Lenin's body now has a waxlike appearance. People sometimes wonder if part or all of the body has been replaced with wax!

Visiting Lenin

Vladimir Lenin was such a strong symbol for the Soviet Union that the government decided the public should be able to continue to see him as such. Lenin's body can be viewed through glass. Chemicals are used to preserve Lenin's remains. The mausoleum is kept at a certain temperature as well. People still wait in long lines to walk through the dark mausoleum. Lenin's tomb is open to visitors most days of the week.

ЛЕНИН

Visitors to Lenin's tomb step down as they enter, walk around the glass coffin, and step up again to exit.

AMERICAN TOMBS

The largest mausoleum in North America is the final resting place of American Civil War general and president Ulysses S. Grant. It's located in Riverside Park in New York City. Two eagle statues guard the outside of the tomb. The words "let us have peace" are written over the entrance—a reminder of the terrible war that divided the country from 1861 to 1865.

Grant's Tomb

In the United States, there are some tombs that hold special significance for the whole nation.

Civil rights movement leader Martin Luther King Jr. is buried in Atlanta, Georgia, at the Martin Luther King Jr. Center for Nonviolent Change. The tomb, which also contains the body of his wife Coretta, lies in the middle of a peaceful pool of water. Near the Kings' tomb, a gas-lit "eternal flame" burns. It serves as a reminder of the murdered leader's constant hope for equality.

Underwater Tomb

When the Japanese bombed Pearl Harbor, Hawaii, on December 7, 1941, the USS *Arizona* battleship was hit four times and sank, killing 1,177 crewmen aboard. It was decided that it would be too difficult to recover the bodies, so the vessel is considered to be a "war grave." Today, a monument has been built over the underwater tomb. Some crewmen who survived the attack have requested that their ashes be buried on the ship after they die.

GRAVE MATTERS

Among those serving on the *Arizona* when it was bombed were 37 sets of brothers.

TOMBS OF TODAY

Some of the modern tombs of today are pretty nice places to hang out. In Egypt, the wealthy don't build pyramids anymore but may buy marble mausoleums with living rooms and even bathrooms inside. Why does a dead person need a bathroom? They don't, but these tombs are made comfortable so the dead's family will enjoy visiting their loved one's resting place. Some mausoleums are rented out as places to live until they're needed!

All over the world, luxury tombs aren't unusual, and some exceed $1 million. Those with views of lakes and other pleasant landscapes are often more expensive. Some people see them as the last house they'll ever purchase, so they request additions like hot tubs and air conditioning.

cremation urns

Cremation

About 42 percent of people today select **cremation** over a burial of the whole body. This isn't a new practice; the ancient Greeks and Romans both favored cremation. Some people want their cremated ashes spread in a favorite place. Others still want them placed in tombs. Many mausoleums have special places to hold cremated remains, which are usually kept in boxes or sealed vases called urns.

Modern mausoleums are usually quiet places where people can sit and visit loved ones who have died.

GRAVE MATTERS

Can you imagine wearing a tomb? Some people get jewelry made of their loved one's ashes.

Many traditions of the past are carried on today when it comes to burials. People are still buried in special ways, hoping to be prepared for an afterlife. Artworks such as effigies and other monuments stand on or near many people's tombs as reminders of who they were and what was special to them. Some people have large mausoleums built for themselves or for their families so they can be together. People are buried in favorite clothes with special items. Sometimes they're buried *in* them. One man in South Carolina chose his favorite car, a 1972 Pontiac Catalina, as his crypt!

GRAVE MATTERS

Some people have chosen to have their cremated remains turned into a reef—a tomb that ocean life can use!

North America

3 12

11

13

Hawaii

South America

No matter what they look like, tombs, crypts, and mausoleums will continue to be sacred spaces, because they're a lasting reminder of and monument to someone's life.

world map key

1 – Dargavs (City of the Dead)
2 – Giza Necropolis
3 – Grave Creek Mound
4 – Lenin's Mausoleum
5 – Newgrange
6 – Nintoku's Tomb
7 – Qin Tomb
8 – Roman Catacombs
9 – Taj Mahal
10 – Tomb of Humayun
11 – Tomb of Martin Luther King Jr.
12 – Tomb of Ulysses S. Grant
13 – U.S.S. *Arizona*
14 – Westminster Abbey

Europe

Asia

Africa

Green Burials

In other ways, burials are changing with the times. For example, some people have "green" burials. They reject the idea of stone tombs and wooden or metal coffins because they don't break down easily underground and may contribute harmful chemicals to the environment. Instead, they choose to be buried in an eco-friendly way, such as in a bamboo casket, so they can more easily become part of nature. There are even special "green" graveyards.

GLOSSARY

archaeologist: a scientist who studies ancient buildings and objects related to past human life and activities

architecture: a style of building, especially one from a certain period of history or a certain place

catacombs: underground passageways and rooms. Sometimes they contain tombs and bones.

civil rights movement: a time period in US history starting in the 1950s in which African Americans fought for equal civil rights, or the freedoms granted by law

communist: someone who practices communism, which is a government system in which the government controls what is used to make and transport products, and there is no privately owned property

cremation: the burning of a dead body until only ashes are left

effigy: a carved representation of someone

excavate: to dig and remove earth in order to find something

mercury: a poisonous silver-white metallic element that is liquid at room temperature

Mesopotamia: an ancient region located between the Tigris and the Euphrates Rivers in what is today Iraq and Syria

Mughal: a member of the Muslim ruling family of Mongol origin that ruled parts of India from 1526 to 1857

symmetry: the property of having an equal balance of something on both sides of a dividing line or around a center

FOR MORE INFORMATION

Books

Malam, John. *Tutankhamun and Other Lost Tombs.* Mankato, MN: QEB Publishing, 2012.

O'Connor, Jane. *Hidden Army: Clay Soldiers of Ancient China.* New York, NY: Grosset & Dunlap, 2011.

Tagliaferro, Linda. *Taj Mahal: India's Majestic Tomb.* New York, NY: Bearport Publishing, 2005.

Websites

Crypts and Catacombs Photos
travel.nationalgeographic.com/travel/countries/crypt-photos/
Check out some creepy and cool photos of skeletons, tombs, and more.

Mausoleum of the First Qin Emperor
whc.unesco.org/en/list/441
Find out more about this jaw-dropping tomb.

Tombs
www.history.com/topics/tombs
Read a short history of tombs and burials.

INDEX